KNOW YOUR GOVERNMENT

The National Park Service

KNOW YOUR GOVERNMENT

The National Park Service

Barry Mackintosh

CHELSEA HOUSE PUBLISHERS
New York • New Haven • Philadelphia

Project Editor: Nancy Priff
Book Editor: Rafaela Ellis
Associate Editor: Linda Fridy
Art Director: Maureen McCafferty
Series Designer: Anita Noble
Chief Copy Editor: Melissa Padovani
Project Coordinator: Kathleen P. Luczak
Editorial Assistant: Constance B. Goodman
Production Manager: Brian A. Shulik
Book Design: Foulk Purvis Design

1 3 5 7 9 8 6 4 2

Library of Congress Cataloging-in-Publication Data

Mackintosh, Barry.
   The National Park Service.
   (Know your government)
   Bibliography:
   Includes index.
   Summary: Examines the history, structure, and function of the National
   Park Service.
   1. United States. National Park Service.
2. National parks and reserves—United States [1. United States. National Park
Service. 2. National parks and reserves.]
I. Title. II. Series: Know your government (New York, N.Y.)
SB482.A4M239   1987   353.0086'32   86-33380

ISBN 1-55546-116-6

ABOUT THE COVER

The National Park Service preserves and protects different types of parks
throughout America. At Yosemite National Park (top) in California, the service
manages the granite peaks and broad meadows of the Sierra Nevada. In the
nation's capital, it runs the Washington Monument (lower left) and many other
features of historical significance. And in Arizona, the service preserves the
world-famous Grand Canyon (lower right) of the Colorado River.

CONTENTS

KNOW YOUR GOVERNMENT

The American Red Cross
The Bureau of Indian Affairs
The Centers for Disease Control
The Central Intelligence Agency
The Children, Youth, and
  Families Division
The Department of Agriculture
The Department of the Air Force
The Department of the Army
The Department of Commerce
The Department of Defense
The Department of Education
The Department of Energy
The Department of Health
  and Human Services
The Department of Housing
  and Urban Development
The Department of the Interior
The Department of Justice
The Department of Labor
The Department of the Navy
The Department of State
The Department of
  Transportation
The Department of the Treasury
The Drug Enforcement
  Administration
The Environmental
  Protection Agency
The Equal Opportunities
  Commission
The Federal Aviation
  Administration
The Federal Bureau of
  Investigation
The Federal Communications
  Commission
The Federal Election Commission

The Federal Railroad
  Administration
The Food and Drug
  Administration
The Food and Nutrition Division
The House of Representatives
The Immigration and
  Naturalization Service
The Internal Revenue Service
The Interstate Commerce
  Commission
The National Foundation on the
  Arts and Humanities
The National Park Service
The National Science Foundation
The Presidency
The Securities and
  Exchange Commission
The Selective Service System
The Senate
The Small Business
  Administration
The Smithsonian
The Supreme Court
The Tennessee Valley Authority
The U.S. Arms Control and
  Disarmament Agency
The U.S. Coast Guard
The U.S. Commission on
  Civil Rights
The U.S. Fish and Wildlife Service
The U.S. Information Agency
The U.S. Mint
The U.S. Nuclear Regulatory
  Commission
The U.S. Postal Service
The U.S. Secret Service
The Veterans Administration

Government: Crises of Confidence

Arthur M. Schlesinger, jr.

From the start, Americans have regarded their government with a mixture of reliance and mistrust. The men who founded the republic did not doubt the indispensability of government. "If men were angels," observed the 51st Federalist Paper, "no government would be necessary." But men are not angels. Since human beings are subject to wicked as well as to noble impulses, government was deemed essential to assure freedom and order.

At the same time, the American revolutionaries knew that government could also become a source of injury and oppression. The men who gathered in Philadelphia in 1787 to write the Constitution therefore had two purposes in mind. They wanted to establish a strong central authority and to limit that central authority's capacity to abuse its power.

To prevent the abuse of power, the founding fathers wrote two basic principles into the new Constitution. The principle of federalism divided power between the state governments and the central authority. The principle of the separation of powers subdivided the central authority itself into three branches—the executive, the legislative, and the judiciary—so that "each may be a check on the other." The *Know Your Government* series focuses on the major executive departments and agencies in these branches of the federal government.

The Constitution did not plan the executive branch in any detail. After vesting the executive power in the president, it assumed the existence of "executive departments" without specifying what these departments should be. Congress began defining their functions in 1789 by creating the Departments of State, Treasury, and War. The secretaries in charge of these departments made up President Washington's first cabinet. Congress also provided for a legal officer, and President Washington soon invited the attorney general, as he was called, to attend cabinet meetings. As need required, Congress created more executive departments.

Setting up the cabinet was only the first step in organizing the American state. With almost no guidance from the Constitution, President Washington, seconded by Alexander Hamilton, his brilliant secretary of the treasury, equipped the infant republic with a working administrative structure. The Federalists believed in both executive energy and executive accountability and set high standards for public appointments. The Jeffersonian opposition had less faith in strong government and preferred local government to the central authority. But when Jefferson himself became president in 1801, although he set out to change the direction of policy, he found no reason to alter the framework the Federalists had erected.

By 1801 there were about 3,000 federal civilian employees in a nation of a little more than 5 million people. Growth in territory and population steadily enlarged national responsibilities. Thirty years later, when Jackson was president, there were more than 11,000 government workers in a nation of 13 million.

The federal establishment was increasing at a faster rate than the population.

Jackson's presidency brought significant changes in the federal service. He believed that the executive branch contained too many officials who saw their jobs as "species of property" and as "a means of promoting individual interest." Against the idea of a permanent service based on life tenure, Jackson argued for the periodic redistribution of federal offices, contending that this was the democratic way and that official duties could be made "so plain and simple that men of intelligence may readily qualify themselves for their performance." He called this policy rotation-in-office. His opponents called it the spoils system.

In fact, partisan legend exaggerated the extent of Jackson's removals. More than 80 percent of federal officeholders retained their jobs. Jackson discharged no larger a proportion of government workers than Jefferson had done a generation earlier. But the rise in these years of mass political parties gave federal patronage new importance as a means of building the party and of rewarding activists. Jackson's successors were less restrained in the distribution of spoils. As the federal establishment grew—to nearly 40,000 by 1861—the politicization of the public service excited increasing concern.

After the Civil War the spoils system became a major political issue. High-minded men condemned it as the root of all political evil. The spoilsmen, said the British commentator James Bryce, "have distorted and depraved the mechanism of politics." Patronage, by giving jobs to unqualified, incompetent, and dishonest persons, lowered the standards of public service and nourished corrupt political machines. Office-seekers pursued presidents and cabinet secretaries without mercy. "Patronage," said Ulysses S. Grant after his presidency, "is the bane of the presidential office." "Every time I appoint someone to office," said another political leader, "I make a hundred enemies

9

and one ingrate." George William Curtis, the president of the National Civil Service Reform League, summed up the indictment. He said,

> The theory which perverts public trusts into party spoils, making public employment dependent upon personal favor and not on proved merit, necessarily ruins the self-respect of public employees, destroys the function of party in a republic, prostitutes elections into a desperate strife for personal profit, and degrades the national character by lowering the moral tone and standard of the country.

The object of civil service reform was to promote efficiency and honesty in the public service and to bring about the ethical regeneration of public life. Over bitter opposition from politicians, the reformers in 1883 passed the Pendleton Act, establishing a bipartisan Civil Service Commission, competitive examinations, and appointment on merit. The Pendleton Act also gave the president authority to extend by executive order the number of "classified" jobs—that is, jobs subject to the merit system. The act applied initially only to about 14,000 of the more than 100,000 federal positions. But by the end of the 19th century 40 percent of federal jobs had moved into the classified category.

Civil service reform was in part a response to the growing complexity of American life. As society grew more organized and problems more technical, official duties were no longer so plain and simple that any person of intelligence could perform them. In public service, as in other areas, the all-round man was yielding ground to the expert, the amateur to the professional. The excesses of the spoils system thus provoked the counterideal of scientific public administration, separate from politics and, as far as possible, insulated against it.

The cult of the expert, however, had its own excesses. The idea that administration could be divorced from policy was an illusion. And in the realm of policy, the expert, however much segregated from partisan politics, can never attain perfect objectivity. He remains the prisoner of his own set of values. It is these values rather than technical expertise that determine fundamental judgments of public policy. To turn over such judgments to experts, moreover, would be to abandon democracy itself; for in a democracy final decisions must be made by the people and their elected representatives. "The business of the expert," the British political scientist Harold Laski rightly said, "is to be on tap and not on top."

Politics, however, were deeply ingrained in American folkways. This meant intermittent tension between the presidential government, elected every four years by the people, and the permanent government, which saw presidents come and go while it went on forever. Sometimes the permanent government knew better than its political masters; sometimes it opposed or sabotaged valuable new initiatives. In the end a strong president with effective cabinet secretaries could make the permanent government responsive to presidential purpose, but it was often an exasperating struggle.

The struggle within the executive branch was less important, however, than the growing impatience with bureaucracy in society as a whole. The 20th century saw a considerable expansion of the federal establishment. The Great Depression and the New Deal led the national government to take on a variety of new responsibilities. The New Deal extended the federal regulatory apparatus. By 1940, in a nation of 130 million people, the number of federal workers for the first time passed the 1 million mark. The Second World War brought federal civilian employment to 3.8 million in 1945. With peace, the federal establishment declined to around 2 million by 1950. Then growth resumed, reaching 2.8 million by the 1980s.

The New Deal years saw rising criticism of "big government" and "bureaucracy." Businessmen resented federal regulation. Conservatives worried about the impact of paternalistic government on individual self-reliance, on community responsibility, and on economic and personal freedom. The nation in effect renewed the old debate between Hamilton and Jefferson in the early republic, although with an ironic exchange of positions. For the Hamiltonian constituency, the "rich and well-born," once the advocate of affirmative government, now condemned government intervention, while the Jeffersonian constituency, the plain people, once the advocate of a weak central government and of states' rights, now favored government intervention.

In the 1980s, with the presidency of Ronald Reagan, the debate has burst out with unusual intensity. According to conservatives, government intervention abridges liberty, stifles enterprise, and is inefficient, wasteful, and arbitrary. It disturbs the harmony of the self-adjusting market and creates worse troubles than it solves. Get government off our backs, according to the popular cliché, and our problems will solve themselves. When government is necessary, let it be at the local level, close to the people. Above all, stop the inexorable growth of the federal government.

In fact, for all the talk about the "swollen" and "bloated" bureaucracy, the federal establishment has not been growing as inexorably as many Americans seem to believe. In 1949, it consisted of 2.1 million people. Thirty years later, while the country had grown by 70 million, the federal force had grown only by 750,000. Federal workers were a smaller percentage of the population in 1985 than they were in 1955—or in 1940. The federal establishment, in short, has not kept pace with population growth. Moreover, national defense and the postal service account for 60 percent of federal employment.

Why then the widespread idea about the remorseless growth of government? It is partly because in the 1960s the national government assumed new and intrusive functions:

affirmative action in civil rights, environmental protection, safety and health in the workplace, community organization, legal aid to the poor. Although this enlargement of the federal regulatory role was accompanied by marked growth in the size of government on all levels, the expansion has taken place primarily in state and local government. Whereas the federal force increased by only 27 percent in the 30 years after 1950, the state and local government force increased by an astonishing 212 percent.

Despite the statistics, the conviction flourishes in some minds that the national government is a steadily growing behemoth swallowing up the liberties of the people. The foes of Washington prefer local government, feeling it is closer to the people and therefore allegedly more responsive to popular needs. Obviously there is a great deal to be said for settling local questions locally. But local government is characteristically the government of the locally powerful. Historically, the way the locally powerless have won their human and constitutional rights has often been through appeal to the national government. The national government has vindicated racial justice against local bigotry, defended the Bill of Rights against local vigilantism, and protected natural resources against local greed. It has civilized industry and secured the rights of labor organizations. Had the states' rights creed prevailed, there would perhaps still be slavery in the United States.

The national authority, far from diminishing the individual, has given most Americans more personal dignity and liberty than ever before. The individual freedoms destroyed by the increase in national authority have been in the main the freedom to deny black Americans their rights as citizens; the freedom to put small children to work in mills and immigrants in sweatshops; the freedom to pay starvation wages, require barbarous working hours, and permit squalid working conditions; the freedom to deceive in the sale of goods and securities; the freedom to pollute the environment—all freedoms that, one supposes, a civilized nation can readily do without.

"Statements are made," said President John F. Kennedy in 1963, "labelling the Federal Government an outsider, an intruder, an adversary. . . . The United States Government is not a stranger or not an enemy. It is the people of fifty states joining in a national effort. . . . Only a great national effort by a great people working together can explore the mysteries of space, harvest the products at the bottom of the ocean, and mobilize the human, natural, and material resources of our lands."

So an old debate continues. However, Americans are of two minds. When pollsters ask large, spacious questions—Do you think government has become too involved in your lives? Do you think government should stop regulating business?—a sizable majority opposes big government. But when asked specific questions about the practical work of government—Do you favor social security? unemployment compensation? Medicare? health and safety standards in factories? environmental protection? government guarantee of jobs for everyone seeking employment? price and wage controls when inflation threatens?—a sizable majority approves of intervention.

In general, Americans do not want less government. What they want is more efficient government. They want government to do a better job. For a time in the 1970s, with Vietnam and Watergate, Americans lost confidence in the national government. In 1964, more than three-quarters of those polled had thought the national government could be trusted to do right most of the time. By 1980 only one-quarter was prepared to offer such trust. But by 1984 trust in the federal government to manage national affairs had climbed back to 45 percent.

Bureaucracy is a term of abuse. But it is impossible to run any large organization, whether public or private, without a bureaucracy's division of labor and hierarchy of authority. And

14

we live in a world of large organizations. Without bureaucracy modern society would collapse. The problem is not to abolish bureaucracy, but to make it flexible, efficient, and capable of innovation.

Two hundred years after the drafting of the Constitution, Americans still regard government with a mixture of reliance and mistrust—a good combination. Mistrust is the best way to keep government reliable. Informed criticism is the means of correcting governmental inefficiency, incompetence, and arbitrariness; that is, of best enabling government to play its essential role. For without government, we cannot attain the goals of the founding fathers. Without an understanding of government, we cannot have the informed criticism that makes government do the job right. It is the duty of every American citizen to *Know Your Government*—which is what this series is all about.

Each year, millions of Americans visit the Grand Canyon and other areas maintained by the National Park Service.

ONE

Preserving America's Parks

What do the Grand Canyon, Statue of Liberty, Mammoth Cave, Washington Monument, Old Faithful geyser, and Liberty Bell have in common? All are famous places or features visited by millions of people every year. All illustrate important aspects of America's natural landscape or human history. And all are part of the National Park System.

To most individuals, the name "National Park Service" conjures up images of Yellowstone National Park and park rangers. But that's only a small part of the total picture. The National Park Service—the federal bureau that manages the National Park System—preserves and protects more than 335 designated areas and keeps them open for the public's enjoyment. These areas are scattered across nearly every state in America, as well as Puerto Rico, the Virgin Islands, and Guam. And they range across the country's history as well as its geography, including pre-Colonial Indian ruins, American Revolution and Civil War battlefields, frontier forts, and homes of 20th-century presidents.

For legislative reasons, Congress has placed the national parks in different categories, although their definitions sometimes overlap. Large parks with spectacular natural features and wilderness usually fall into the national park category. Yellowstone National Park, the site of Old Faithful, is a well-known national park that covers territory in Wyoming, Montana, and Idaho.

The Liberty Bell is displayed in a national historical park—a park that honors important people, events, or artifacts.

The national monuments category includes areas with at least one resource of national importance. Usually smaller than national parks, national monuments include the Natural Bridges National Monument in Utah and man-made features, such as the Statue of Liberty in New York Harbor.

As suggested by the name, the national historical parks category includes areas and features of historical significance, such as Independence National Historical Park in Philadelphia, home of the Liberty Bell and Independence Hall. These parks are usually larger and more complex than national historic sites, which also commemorate people and events important in American history. Usually small in area, the sites commonly contain a single primary feature—for example, Abraham Lincoln's home in Springfield, Illinois.

National military parks include many battlefields, such as the site of a Revolutionary War battle at Kings Mountain, South Carolina, and the Civil War battlefield at Gettysburg, Pennsylvania.

National seashores, lakeshores, rivers, and recreational areas protect land near bodies of water and ensure public access for recreation. These categories include shore areas along the Great Lakes as well as Lake Mead, formed by the Hoover Dam between Arizona and Nevada.

National parkways and scenic trails are two other park service categories. Designed for scenic touring rather than high-speed travel, they include the Appalachian Trail—a 2,100-mile- (3,360-kilometer-) long trail that runs from Maine to Georgia— and the Blue Ridge Parkway in Virginia and North Carolina.

Most Americans probably will visit one of these areas sometime during their lives. Although they may quickly recognize the rangers who work in the parks, they may not be aware of the many people working behind-the-scenes to keep the areas presentable, safe, and enjoyable. And they may not be familiar with the story of the National Park Service—a tale of dedication to America's environment and its people.

Early pioneers took pride in taming the wilderness. Later Americans valued the preservation of land and wildlife.

TWO

Before the National Park Service

The national parks grew out of the changes in America's attitude toward expansion in the 19th century. In 1800, most Americans lived in rural areas. To most of them, the unsettled western land seemed limitless. It did not occur to them to set parts of it aside to be kept free from settlement, logging, or other development. They wanted to conquer and tame the plentiful wilderness, not preserve it. The farmers, miners, and ranchers regarded the frontier as an obstacle to overcome.

But others began to feel differently. Most of them came from the East, where cities had mushroomed and farms had spread across the land, taking over much of the wilderness. They thought America was losing something valuable—the vast, uncultivated lands and wildlife that distinguished it from many older nations.

One such man was George Catlin, an artist with a special interest in the Native Americans, or Indians. In 1832, while on a

Catlin's paintings celebrated the Indian life that he hoped parks would protect.

trip to what is now South Dakota, Catlin observed that the frontier's advance was threatening the wild buffalo and the Indians who depended on buffalo meat and hides. His observations prompted an idea that he wrote in his journal, which was published as a book in 1841. He stated that the decline of wildlife and Indian civilization might be halted if they were "by some great protecting policy of the government preserved . . . in a *magnificent park. . . . A nation's park*, containing man and beast, in all the wildness and freshness of their nature's beauty!"

Nothing came of Catlin's idea just then, although in that same year Congress decided to keep a special piece of government land. This was the Hot Springs Reservation in the Arkansas Territory, where 47 hot springs thought to have curative powers emerged from the base of a mountain. Instead of selling this land, the government leased it to businessmen, who developed it as a resort rather than preserving it in its natural condition. They built hotels and bathhouses for travelers who came to drink and bathe in the mineral waters.

The First National Parks

The federal government didn't act to preserve a large natural area until 1864. In that year, President Abraham Lincoln signed a law that gave the spectacular, federally owned Yosemite Valley to the state of California to be managed as a state park. If California had been a federal territory rather than a state at the time, Yosemite might have been the first national park. Instead, that honor went to Yellowstone.

Yellowstone became the second large natural area that the federal government set aside for preservation. In the mid-1800s, only a few trappers and other frontiersmen knew of the Yellowstone region. And their colorful tales of boiling pools and erupting geysers often met with disbelief. But between 1869 and 1871 three government-sponsored expeditions confirmed these stories

Yellowstone's geysers and other wonders prompted Congress to make it the first national park, in 1872.

with scientific descriptions, photographs, and paintings of the thermal phenomena, the Yellowstone's Grand Canyon, and other scenic features. Publicity about these findings aroused great public interest in Yellowstone's natural wonders.

Some individuals may have desired private ownership of Yellowstone's geysers and other features, but many others believed that such a special place should not belong to only a few. With the help of railroad companies, which would profit from tourism to the area, they successfully campaigned to have Congress declare Yellowstone "reserved and withdrawn from settlement, occupancy, or sale . . . and dedicated and set apart as a public park . . . for the benefit and enjoyment of the people." On March 1, 1872, President Ulysses S. Grant signed the law establishing Yellowstone National Park.

The Department of the Interior was responsible for most of the government's western land, including the Yellowstone area, and it remained in charge when Yellowstone became a national park. Because park supporters claimed that income from leasing sites for hotels and other tourist accommodations would pay for improving and protecting Yellowstone, for several years Congress gave the department no extra money to manage the park. But the park's income proved inadequate, and Yellowstone developed other problems, too. Squatters moved in and illegally occupied portions of the land. Poachers killed buffalo, elk, and other wildlife. And thoughtless tourists damaged some of the mineral formations at the geysers, hot springs, and other areas.

So Secretary L.Q.C. Lamar, head of the Department of the Interior, called in the United States Army to patrol Yellowstone in 1886. For the next 30 years, horse-mounted cavalry troops maintained law and order there. During this period, army engineers constructed buildings to house the soldiers and built roads and trails to improve travel in the park.

In 1890, Congress set up three more national parks, all in California. Two parks—Sequoia National Park and General Grant

Glacier National Park joined the system in the early 1900s.

National Park (now part of Kings Canyon National Park)—were designated to protect groves of giant sequoia trees. The third, Yosemite National Park, was established to preserve the high sierra country above Yosemite Valley. (In 1906, the federal government included the valley in the national park as well.) Because the Interior Department lacked the funds, staff, and equipment for these parks, it again asked the army to patrol them and construct improvements.

As the idea of national parks became more popular, Congress set aside still more of America's western wonderlands. Parks created during the early 1900s included Crater Lake National Park in Oregon, where a blue lake rests in an ancient volcanic mountain; Glacier National Park in Montana, where nearly 50 glaciers lie amid lakes and mountains; Rocky Mountain National Park in Colorado, one of the most scenic areas of the Rockies; Lassen Volcanic National Park in California, where Lassen Peak erupted in 1914; and Hawaii National Park (now Hawaii Volcanoes National Park) in Hawaii.

The First National Monuments

In the late 1800s, citizens became concerned about protecting cliff dwellings and other prehistoric Indian ruins on government land in the Southwest. Collectors and sellers of pottery and artifacts had been disturbing these valuable archaeological sites. So in 1889, Congress authorized the president to protect one such site—the large Casa Grande ruin in Arizona—from settlement or sale. But the number of similar archaeological sites made it impractical for Congress to pass separate laws protecting each one.

As a result, Congress passed the Antiquities Act of 1906. It allowed the president to reserve as national monuments "historic

The Antiquities Act protected these ancient cliff dwellings.

In 1906, Devils Tower became the first national monument.

landmarks, historic and prehistoric structures, and other objects of historic and scientific interest" on the public lands. It also set penalties for excavating ruins and taking artifacts without permission.

On September 24, 1906, President Theodore Roosevelt proclaimed the first national monument: Devils Tower, a massive stone shaft looming above northeastern Wyoming. A guidepost for Indians, explorers, and settlers, this eerie volcanic tower was most significant as a natural feature. So were many of the national monuments that followed, such as the Petrified Forest in Arizona, with its ancient wood transformed into colorful stone; Muir Woods in California, with its coastal redwood trees; and Rainbow Bridge in Utah, the world's largest natural stone arch.

Other national monuments protected prehistoric ruins and historic places. On December 8, 1906, Roosevelt proclaimed the first two of these types: Montezuma Castle, Arizona, one of the best-preserved Indian cliff dwellings; and El Morro, New Mexico, where prehistoric Indians, 17th-century Spanish explorers, and 19th-century American settlers left hundreds of carvings on Inscription Rock.

Some national monuments matched national parks in size and scenic quality, and some of these later became national parks, such as the famous Grand Canyon of Arizona and the Petrified Forest National Monument. Other large national monuments, such as Death Valley in California and Nevada, have kept that designation.

Some national monuments, such as Fort Sumter, South Carolina, where the Civil War began, were established by acts of Congress rather than by presidential proclamations. Because Congress was more likely to provide money for national monuments that it had created, park supporters favored this method of establishment in later years.

In addition to lands held by the Department of the Interior, the president soon created national monuments on lands administered by the Departments of War and Agriculture. These monuments included some of the War Department's historic forts and several of the Agriculture Department's prehistoric Indian sites

Congress established Fort Sumter National Monument, where visitors can see cannons and other Civil War memorabilia.

In 1915, Stephen T. Mather accepted the challenge to improve park conditions.

and geologic features. At first, these departments did little to care for most of their national monuments. Many people expected the Interior Department to improve the management of these monuments and their surrounding parkland, because it was responsible for so many others.

Among those who sought to improve this situation was Stephen T. Mather, a wealthy Chicago businessman who loved hiking and climbing in the parks. In 1914, Mather wrote to his friend, Secretary of the Interior Franklin K. Lane, to complain about the way the parks were being run. Lane replied that if Mather was dissatisfied he should come to Washington and run them himself.

Mather couldn't resist the challenge. The following year he began work as a special assistant to Secretary Lane in charge of park matters. Horace M. Albright, a young Californian who had joined the Interior Department in 1913, became Mather's right-hand man.

Mather and Albright found the parks and monuments operating with little coordination, as if each existed by itself. The army ran some of the parks, civilians operated others, and part-time employees took care of many of the monuments. In addition, none of the parks had sufficient funding to hire enough good employees, to build needed roads, and to serve visitors well while protecting park features. Mather felt that these problems would continue as long as the Interior Department had no bureau devoted to the parks and monuments. He envisioned such a bureau not only to run these areas, but also to publicize and build public support for them. He believed that Congress would supply more money for parks and monuments once it saw that they were in good hands and that people were eager to visit them.

For several years park supporters had tried to get Congress to establish a national park bureau. Mather and Albright took over this campaign with great skill and enthusiasm. Mather published a fine picture book on the parks, which he sent to every member of Congress. In 1915, he and Albright took a group of congressmen, journalists, and other influential citizens on a trip through Sequoia and Yosemite national parks, gaining their support and winning publicity in magazines such as *National Geographic*. Back in Washington, Albright won over other members of Congress.

Their campaign succeeded. On August 25, 1916, President Woodrow Wilson signed a law creating the National Park Service within the Department of the Interior. This law, known as the Organic Act, gave the new service responsibility for the 14 national parks and 21 national monuments then managed by the department, as well as Hot Springs Reservation and "such other national parks and reservations of like character as may be hereafter created by Congress."

A particularly significant part of the act was the way it defined the purpose of caring for the parks and monuments. It instructed the service "to conserve the scenery and the natural and historic objects and the wild life therein and to provide for the enjoyment of the same in such manner and by such means as will leave them unimpaired for the enjoyment of future generations." In other words, the service could let people enjoy these areas only in ways that would not damage or use up the features that made them special. For example, visitors to the Petrified Forest would have to enjoy the park without collecting samples of petrified wood, because if they did, there would be nothing left for their great-grandchildren to see. Visitors to Mesa Verde National Park in Colorado could not climb over its prehistoric cliff dwellings, because they could destroy the fragile ruins. Construction of roads, hotels, campgrounds, and restaurants in the parks would have to be controlled, because too much development would spoil the natural atmosphere. Preserving park features while letting people enjoy them would be the service's biggest challenge.

Mather (left) and Albright (right) directed the park service after Congress passed the Organic Act in 1916.

THREE

Building the Foundations

In the early years, two men set the tone and direction for the new National Park Service—Stephen T. Mather and Horace Albright. They established a park management system, setting general policies and applying them to all areas. And they laid the foundation for today's park system—both the quantity of its area and the quality of its care.

Stephen T. Mather had planned to return to his business as soon as Congress passed the Organic Act. But Secretary Lane appointed Mather the service's first director and persuaded him to remain long enough to get it started. (He actually stayed for 12 years.) As director, Mather continued to be a great salesman for the parks, encouraging people to visit and appreciate their wonders, persuading Congress to increase funding, and donating much of his personal fortune to pay for roads, buildings, and other park needs.

Horace Albright had not planned to stay, either, but he too fell in love with the parks and accepted the job of assistant director. In 1919, he moved west to become superintendent of Yellowstone National Park. He followed Mather as director in 1929 and stayed until 1933, when he left for a job in private industry. But he remained deeply interested in the parks and offered advice to his successors for more than 50 years.

A 1918 letter to Director Mather (composed by Albright and signed by Secretary Lane) outlined policies, or instructions, on how the National Park System was to be developed and administered. The service still tries to follow many of these policies today. One called for special care in park development: "In the construction of roads, trails, buildings, and other improvements, particular attention must be devoted always to the harmonizing of these improvements with the landscape." Another encouraged

According to Albright, trails had to blend with the landscape.

park museums and other programs to explain and exhibit specimens of natural features.

Still another had to do with the growth of the system. Lane told Mather to ". . . seek . . . scenery of supreme and distinctive quality or some natural feature so extraordinary or unique as to be of national interest and importance. . . . The national park system . . . should not be lowered in standard, dignity, and prestige by the inclusion of areas which express in less than the highest terms the particular class or kind of exhibit which they represent."

Mather and Albright tried to hire only the most highly qualified park rangers and superintendents. They tried to find people who knew how to care for the parks and, just as important, how to get along well with park visitors. They also had to find qualified park naturalists who could plan interpretive programs and present them to visitors, telling them about the park's wildlife, trees, flowers, and geology in campfire talks, guided walks, booklets, and museum and trailside exhibits. This communication helped protect park features, because visitors who learned to appreciate them were usually careful not to harm them.

When it began operation, the National Park Service was responsible for only one area east of the Mississippi River, a national monument in Maine that would later become Acadia National Park. Because most of the nation's population lived in the East, Mather was sure he could increase park support by adding more eastern areas to the park system. He was delighted, therefore, when Congress passed laws in 1926 authorizing Great Smoky Mountains National Park on the Tennessee-North Carolina border, Shenandoah National Park in Virginia's Blue Ridge Mountains, and Mammoth Cave National Park in Kentucky.

Unlike most of the western parks and monuments, these eastern parks were not on land owned by the federal government, and for many years Congress was unwilling to spend money to buy parklands. As a result, these parks could be established only after state governments or private citizens acquired the lands and donated them to the federal government. John D. Rockefeller, Jr., was especially generous in buying and then donating land for several parks, including Acadia, Great Smoky Mountains, and Grand Teton National Park in Wyoming.

Albright shared Mather's desire to build up the National Park System in the East. He was also interested in American history and knew that the East had many historic places that were suitable for national parks. The War Department already administered some of them as national military parks and national monuments, such as Revolutionary War and Civil War battlefields. But Albright thought the National Park Service should manage them.

When he tried to get Congress to transfer these historical parks to his bureau, his opponents argued that the park service had no experience managing areas of that kind. Albright overcame this argument in the early 1930s by acquiring three new historical parks for the service: George Washington's birthplace

Maine's Acadia National Park was once the only eastern park.

Washington's birthplace became a historical park in 1930.

in Virginia, Colonial National Monument in Virginia, and Morristown National Historical Park in New Jersey. Colonial National Monument (later made a national historical park) included Jamestown Island, site of the first permanent English settlement in America, and Yorktown Battlefield, scene of the last battle of the Revolutionary War. Morristown was the headquarters for Washington's army for two winters during that war. Albright hired the first service historians to help develop these areas and interpret their stories for visitors.

Albright's greatest opportunity arose soon after Franklin D. Roosevelt became president in March 1933. By good fortune, he was assigned to ride in Roosevelt's car on a drive from Shenandoah National Park to Washington, D.C. On the way they passed through a Civil War battlefield, and Albright told the president about the War Department's parks and explained how the park

*An interest in parks spurred Roosevelt (left) to grant more
properties to the National Park Service.*

service might better manage them. Roosevelt liked his plan and
told him to get to work on the details. So Albright helped prepare
a presidential order that would carry out his plan, and Roosevelt
signed it on June 10, 1933.

Suddenly, the park service had a windfall of new properties.
The order gave the service not only the War Department's parks
and monuments, but also the Agriculture Department's national
monuments and the great stone monuments and memorials in
Washington, D.C. From the War Department came Revolutionary War battlefields, such as Guilford Courthouse National Military Park, North Carolina, and Kings Mountain National Military
Park, South Carolina; Civil War battlefields, including Shiloh National Military Park, Tennessee, and Vicksburg National Military
Park, Mississippi; and national monuments, such as Fort Pulaski,
Georgia, and the Statue of Liberty. From the Agriculture De-

partment came prehistoric ruins, including those at Walnut Canyon National Monument, Arizona, and natural features, such as the caverns of Lehman Caves National Monument, Nevada. From the Office of Public Buildings and Public Parks of the National Capital came the Washington Monument, the Lincoln Memorial, Ford's Theatre (where President Lincoln was assassinated), Arlington House (home of Robert E. Lee), and other historic sites and parklands around Washington, D.C.

This 1933 transfer of parks was the greatest event ever to befall the National Park Service. All at once, the park system grew by a dozen natural areas and nearly 50 historical areas. Some of them, such as the forts and memorials, were unlike anything the service had managed before. They broadened the concept of the park system and encouraged similar additions in the future. They also changed the service from a bureau with a western emphasis to a truly national one.

After 1933, the park service began to administer miles of beaches and other recreation areas for natural entertainment.

FOUR

Growth and
New Directions

Over the next 30 years the
National Park System continued to grow, adding 93 new areas.
Only 14 of these were natural parks. As wilderness became scar-
cer, fewer places that qualified as national parklands were available. The number of historical areas leapt by 66, and these were
joined by 13 sites in the newly created category of recreational
areas.

This new category broadened the scope of the service, and
so did the nature of the additions to existing categories. One
such addition was Everglades National Park in southern Florida,
containing the largest tropical wilderness in the United States. It
is well-known for its alligators and many species of birds. Chan-
nel Islands National Monument was another unusual addition. It
protected two beautiful islands off the southern California coast.
The Virgin Islands National Park also expanded the service's
scope, covering most of the land and offshore waters of St. John
Island in the Caribbean Sea.

Everglades Park provided a natural habitat for tropical birds.

Many of the new historical additions were encouraged by the Historic Sites Act of 1935. In this act, Congress declared "a national policy to preserve for public use historic sites, buildings, and objects of national significance for the inspiration and benefit of the people of the United States." Most historical areas came to the park system by separate acts of Congress, but the Historic Sites Act permitted the National Park Service to recommend suitable additions. It also authorized the service to restore historic buildings, to build museums, and to conduct educational programs at its historic places.

Many of the new areas became national historic sites. Among them was Fort Raleigh National Historic Site, North Carolina, where England tried to establish its first settlement in North America in 1585. Here the park service uncovered buried artifacts from the settlement and rebuilt the earthen fort as an exhibit. Fort Davis National Historic Site contains many of the original buildings from that 19th-century army post on the Texas frontier. Sagamore Hill National Historic Site at Oyster Bay, New York, once the beautiful home of Theodore Roosevelt, is furnished much as he left it. Edison National Historic Site in West Orange, New Jersey, encompasses Thomas Edison's home and laboratory.

Independence National Historical Park in Philadelphia— where the nation's founding fathers adopted the Declaration of Independence and wrote the Constitution—joined the National Park System in 1948. Other additions during this period included the 185-mile (296-kilometer) Chesapeake and Ohio Canal along the Potomac River, and the home of Frederick Douglass, the most famous 19th-century black abolitionist, in Washington, D.C.

Besides these sites and buildings of national significance, the service found many others that were not available for addition to the park system because they were held by other federal agencies, state and local governments, private organizations, and individuals. Since 1960, secretaries of the interior have designated more than 1,700 of them as national historic landmarks, including Mount Vernon, George Washington's home; Monticello, Thomas Jefferson's home; and the Alamo mission in San Antonio, Texas. Owners of landmarks who agree to preserve them receive bronze plaques to display, stating the national significance of these properties.

The new category of recreational areas included several types of parks intended to serve many visitors. After the Interior Department's Bureau of Reclamation completed Hoover Dam on the Colorado River in 1935, the service built and operated campgrounds, boat launching ramps, and other public facilities on Lake Mead, the huge reservoir behind the dam. Lake Mead National

Although it was not owned by the federal government, the Alamo was designated as a national historic landmark.

Recreational Area was the first and remains the largest such unit of the National Park System. Others include Coulee Dam National Recreation Area in Washington and Glen Canyon National Recreation Area in Arizona and Utah.

Recreational areas also included man-made national parkways. The service acquired the first of these in 1933: George Washington Memorial Parkway, a scenic drive from Washington, D.C., to Mount Vernon, Virginia. Soon afterward it began work on the Blue Ridge Parkway in Virginia and North Carolina, extending 469 miles (750.4 kilometers) between the Shenandoah and Great Smoky Mountains national parks. Almost as long is the Natchez Trace Parkway, following an old trail between Nashville, Tennessee, and Natchez, Mississippi. The service carefully designed and landscaped these parkways to maximize sightseeing.

In 1937, Congress passed a law to establish Cape Hatteras as a national seashore; it stretches along almost 100 miles (160 kilometers) of barrier-island beach on the North Carolina coast. Twenty-four years later, Congress established a second national seashore, in Cape Cod. Later national seashores included Padre Island, Texas, and Point Reyes, California. Although these seashores serve large numbers of recreational beachgoers, they also keep portions of the coastline in their natural state, free from private development.

The Great Depression of the 1930s was a difficult time for many Americans, but the National Park Service benefitted from government programs intended to reduce the widespread unemployment of those years. One such program was the Civilian Conservation Corps, which hired thousands of young men to construct roads, trails, buildings, and campgrounds and make other

Cape Hatteras became a national seashore in 1937.

The Civilian Conservation Corps restored this house in 1937.

park improvements. Some of their efforts are still in evidence, including restored canal locks on the Chesapeake and Ohio Canal and stone walls on the Gettysburg battlefield.

The park service faced greater problems during the World War II years of 1941 to 1945. While America dedicated its resources to the war, little money was available for the parks. And lumber and mining companies, ranchers, and others wanted to use the parks for logging, mining, livestock grazing, and other damaging activities that they argued were needed to support the war.

After the war, proposals for large dams threatened to flood wilderness canyons in some parks. However, Newton B. Drury, director of the service during the 1940s, successfully defended the parks against most of these threats. When travel to the parks increased greatly after the war, another problem became apparent. Many of the improvements made during the 1930s had deteriorated or were inadequate to serve all the new visitors. In 1956, Director Conrad L. Wirth began a ten-year program to correct this situation. It was called MISSION 66, because it was to be completed in time for the park service's 50th anniversary in 1966. Nearly every park received new or improved facilities; the visitor center buildings and employee houses currently in use in many parks were constructed during MISSION 66.

Although most people welcomed these improvements, some complained that the service was overdeveloping the parks, violating its responsibility to "leave them unimpaired for the enjoyment of future generations." The Wilderness Society and other conservation organizations influenced Congress to pass the Wilderness Act of 1964. Under this law, Congress and the president have set aside many large, undeveloped sections of the parks as permanent wilderness areas where no roads, buildings, or other facilities can be constructed.

After the early 1960s, the National Park System entered a period of renewed, and even faster, growth. In fact, it acquired 145 of its 337 units between 1963 and 1986. Nearly half were historical areas, and many others were recreational areas. The number of natural parks also increased significantly because of Alaska—America's last great source of wilderness.

The new historical parks included many homes of United States presidents, such as Martin Van Buren, Abraham Lincoln, William Howard Taft, Herbert Hoover, Harry S. Truman, Dwight D. Eisenhower, John F. Kennedy, and Lyndon B. Johnson. By 1986, parks or national historic landmarks existed for all but the most recent presidents.

Military history offered important additions, too. Andersonville National Historic Site in Georgia bears witness to the story of a notorious Civil War prison camp there. Boston National Historical Park contains the Bunker Hill Monument, near the place where British and American forces clashed during the Revolution, and the Boston Naval Shipyard, home of the legendary

To commemorate World War II, Congress established this floating memorial to the crew of the battleship Arizona.

U.S.S. *Constitution*, or "Old Ironsides," a navy warship that fought in the War of 1812. Valley Forge, Pennsylvania, site of the famous Revolutionary War encampment, became a national historical park on July 4, 1976. Two new parks commemorate World War II: U.S.S. *Arizona* Memorial at Pearl Harbor, Hawaii, where the service operates a visitor center over the sunken battleship; and War in the Pacific National Historical Park on the island of Guam, the scene of heavy combat.

Congress established parks for other aspects of American history as well. The homes of John Muir, Carl Sandburg, Henry Wadsworth Longfellow, Edgar Allan Poe, and Eugene O'Neill became national historic sites recognizing the literary and dramatic contributions of these important writers. Saugus Iron Works National Historic Site, Springfield Armory National Historic Site, and Lowell National Historical Park, all in Massachusetts, deal with manufacturing industries from the 17th to the 20th centuries. Tuskegee Institute National Historic Site, Alabama, contains part of the industrial school for blacks that Booker T. Washington established in 1881. Clara Barton National Historic Site in Maryland, home of the founder of the American Red Cross, and Eleanor Roosevelt National Historic Site, Mrs. Roosevelt's retreat at Hyde Park, New York, were among several new parks honoring famous American women.

Four national lakeshores on the Great Lakes joined the national seashores during this period: Pictured Rocks and Sleeping Bear Dunes in Michigan, Indiana Dunes in Indiana, and Apostle Islands in Wisconsin. In 1964, Congress established the first of several river parks, Ozark National Scenic Riverways in Missouri. Later river parks included New River Gorge National River, West Virginia, and Rio Grande Wild and Scenic River, Texas. Rafting, canoeing, and kayaking are popular recreational activities in these areas. The 2,000-mile- (3,200-kilometer-) long Appalachian Trail became part of the National Park System in 1968. Although it is not the largest park, it is certainly the longest!

Congress established two recreational areas serving large cities in 1972. Gateway National Recreation Area in New York City and nearby New Jersey includes beaches, historic fortifications, and a wildlife refuge. Golden Gate National Recreation Area, in and near San Francisco, contains a redwood forest, marshes, historic ships and forts, and Alcatraz Island, with its infamous prison. In later years, Congress added other urban recreation areas to the system.

Several natural areas joined the system as national parks, beginning in 1964 with Canyonlands National Park in southeastern Utah, a geological wonderland of rocks, spires, and mesas. North Cascades National Park, Washington, with its jagged peaks, lakes, and glaciers, and Redwood National Park, California, containing the world's tallest trees, were established together in 1968. In 1974, Congress passed laws creating the first

Congress established Big Thicket and other natural preserves that differ from parks because they allow hunting.

two national preserves: Big Cypress National Preserve, Florida, and Big Thicket National Preserve, Texas. These areas, rich in plant and animal life, resemble national parks, but because they allow hunting and other activities prohibited in national parks, Congress gave them a new name to distinguish them.

In 1973, the National Park System contained about 13 million acres (5.2 million hectares) of land. Then Secretary of the Interior Rogers C.B. Morton recommended that 32 million acres (12.8 million hectares) of government land in Alaska be set aside as national parks and monuments, in addition to the Alaskan parkland already in existence. The proposal was quite controversial. Conservationists favored even more protected parkland, whereas many Alaskans opposed putting so much land out of reach of mining, hunting, and other interests forbidden in national parks. Congress debated the subject for years before passing the Alaska National Interest Lands Conservation Act of 1980.

Secretary Morton caused controversy with his Alaska plan.

This single act enlarged the system by more than 47 million acres (18.8 million hectares), making it 2.5 times larger than before. The combined territory of the national parklands—more than 124,000 square miles (322,400 square kilometers)—was now larger than all but four individual states (Alaska, Texas, California, and Montana). Alaska now had 23 areas, more than any other state: 8 national parks, 2 national monuments, 2 national historical parks, 1 wild river, and 10 national preserves that permitted hunting and trapping—part of a compromise with the park opponents.

The Alaska parks include the system's largest unit, Wrangell-St. Elias National Park, containing 14,000 square miles (36,000 square kilometers)—more than Maryland, Delaware, and

The Wrangell-St. Elias National Park in Alaska added vast expanses of wilderness to the park system.

Rhode Island combined—and the greatest collection of peaks above 16,000 feet (4,800 meters) in North America. Denali National Park boasts the highest point in the United States, 20,320-foot (6,096-meter) Mount McKinley. Noatak National Preserve, the northernmost area of the system, lies entirely above the Arctic Circle. Its untouched river basin is the largest in the United States and contains an array of animals and plants as well as prehistoric archaeological sites.

As director of the service from 1964 through 1972, George B. Hartzog, Jr., was responsible for much of this growth. Some of his successors, especially Director Russell E. Dickenson (1980–1985), thought the service had acquired more parks than it could properly care for and tried to slow the system's growth. After 1980, Congress generally agreed with this view and created few new parks. Instead, it appropriated more than $1 billion for the service's five-year Park Restoration and Improvement Program, which repaired and upgraded existing park facilities.

In addition to all its new parks, the service assumed other responsibilities as well. One was a program to identify and help protect natural places of national significance outside the system, similar to the national historic landmarks program for historic places. Secretary of the Interior Stewart L. Udall designated the first national natural landmarks in 1964. By 1986, nearly 600 natural landmarks stretched from Mount Katahdin, Maine, to Diamond Head, Hawaii.

In 1916, the National Park Service had 36 areas to manage. Most were national parks and monuments in the West. Within 70 years it had custody of 337 areas—including wilderness parks, historic sites, and urban recreation areas—throughout the entire nation, and concerns including natural and historic places outside the National Park System. The tremendous growth of the system and its added responsibilities required the bureau to grow along with it.

In addition to its famous rangers, the park service employs specialists in a variety of fields, including the sciences.

FIVE

Today's Park Service Organization

Thousands of National Park Service employees manage the day-to-day activities in parks across the nation. Many other employees work at the bureau's headquarters, administering the park system and working closely with other branches of the government. Both parts of the organization work together to operate one of the world's largest national park systems.

The National Park Service is part of the Department of the Interior, which is headed by the secretary of the interior, a member of the president's cabinet. His or her cabinet position makes the department part of the executive (presidential) branch of the government. The department's primary purpose is to manage most of the government's land. Several assistant secretaries report to the secretary of the interior, including the assistant secretary for fish and wildlife and parks. This assistant secretary supervises the directors of the National Park Service and the United States Fish and Wildlife Service.

The National Park Service headquarters, located in the Interior Building in Washington, D.C., houses the director and his staff. The park service director plans and controls the bureau's activities. He is appointed by the secretary of the interior, but unlike many other bureau heads, he is not automatically replaced

Part of the Department of the Interior, the park service is headquartered in the Interior Building in Washington, D.C.

whenever a president of a different political party comes to office. This has been true because the Democrats and the Republicans have not differed significantly in their approach to running the parks. Most directors have strong backgrounds in park management.

The deputy director reports to the director, shares many of his duties, and acts as director in his absence. The secretary of the interior also appoints the deputy director, who has usually spent his career in the service.

Several offices and their staffs advise and assist the director and deputy director. The Office of Legislative and Congressional Affairs helps Congress write park-related bills, prepares recommendations on bills, and deals with Congress in many other ways. The Office of Public Affairs provides information about parks and the service to the media and the public. It operates an information office stocked with booklets and folders on the parks. The special assistant for policy development prepares and distributes the park management policies that all park superintendents must follow. His office reviews park plans to see that they do not violate the policies. The equal opportunity officer ensures that the service selects and promotes its employees without regard to their race, sex, religion, or ethnic background. The Office of Business and Economic Development helps businesses owned by women and members of racial minorities to obtain contracts and concessions with the service.

The associate director for cultural resources develops policies and programs for studying, preserving, and using the cultural resources of the parks—the prehistoric and historic sites, structures, and objects. His staff also keeps the National Register of Historic Places, supervises programs to preserve these properties, evaluates proposed historical parks, and selects places to become national historic landmarks.

The associate director for natural resources oversees activities that preserve the parks' natural features. He supervises the

The National Park Service Headquarters Organization

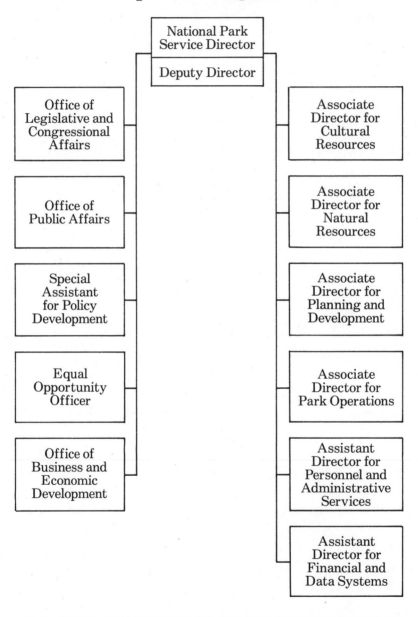

National Park Service Director

Deputy Director

Office of Legislative and Congressional Affairs

Office of Public Affairs

Special Assistant for Policy Development

Equal Opportunity Officer

Office of Business and Economic Development

Associate Director for Cultural Resources

Associate Director for Natural Resources

Associate Director for Planning and Development

Associate Director for Park Operations

Assistant Director for Personnel and Administrative Services

Assistant Director for Financial and Data Systems

senior scientist, who gathers scientific information on the parks and uses it to care for their biological, botanical, and geological resources. He also oversees divisions responsible for studying and safeguarding park air and water quality and for seeing that mining activities permitted in and around certain parks do as little damage as possible.

The associate director for planning and development is responsible for all National Park System plans, proposed park studies, and major construction projects. His staff must also review other federal agencies' plans to consider their impact on park areas.

The associate director for park operations is responsible for matters involving park management, maintenance, interpretation, ranger activities, safety, and concessions—private businesses in the parks that provide accommodations, food, and other services. His Visitor Services Division deals with interpretive and other programs, law enforcement, and other functions related to public use of the parks.

The assistant director for personnel and administrative services and the assistant director for financial and data systems handle "housekeeping" chores. Their divisions order supplies, hire and pay employees, arrange contracts with private businesses, prepare the service's annual budget, and pay its bills. Part of the Personnel and Administrative Services staff supervises the park service training centers at Harpers Ferry National Historical Park, West Virginia, and at Grand Canyon National Park, Arizona. Courses at these centers introduce new employees to the service and train other employees in park management skills.

The service is divided into ten regions: North Atlantic, Mid-Atlantic, National Capital, Southeast, Midwest, Rocky Mountain, Southwest, Western, Pacific Northwest, and Alaska. A regional director heads each one and reports to the park service director. Park superintendents report to the director for their area. Most

Regions of the National Park Service

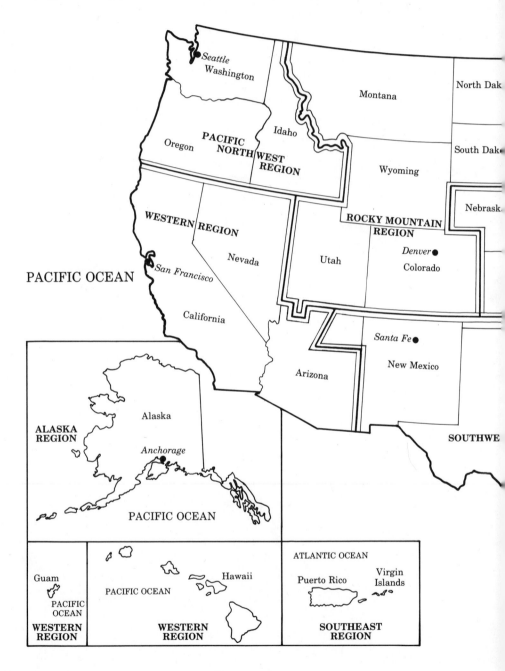

LEGEND

Regional Offices   •

Regional Boundaries   ═══

regions cover several states and each has an office in a major city.

Each regional office is similar to the Washington office. The regional director is responsible for the parks and service activities in the territory. A deputy regional director shares the director's work and stands in when he or she is absent. Associate regional directors advise and assist the deputy and regional directors.

The park superintendents are key people in the park service—like ship captains in the navy. The parks form the hub of the service, and their superintendents are directly responsible for preserving their features and making them available for public enjoyment. Most superintendents join the service as rangers or other service employees.

In a large park, the superintendent's staff may include an assistant superintendent and several divisions, each headed by a chief and specializing in one of the following areas: care of the park's natural and historic features, interpretation of them for visitors, law enforcement and protection, park facility maintenance, or administrative duties, such as hiring employees and purchasing equipment. A small park does many of the same things, but with a much smaller staff, so that each person must perform a wider range of duties. Because a small park may lack specialists in areas such as wildlife management and historic building repair, its superintendent often must seek help from the regional office.

The service employs people with many skills for many different jobs. Rangers, whose duties extend from law enforcement to fire prevention to nature interpretation, usually have college degrees in natural science, park and recreation management, history, or some other park-related field. Other employees include biologists, architects, engineers, archaeologists, research historians, management specialists, computer programmers, writers, land appraisers, museum specialists, recreation planners, admin-

A ranger's many responsibilities include greeting visitors, supplying information, and enforcing park regulations.

istrative officers, maintenance workers, and secretaries. Many of these positions also require a college degree, and some require graduate school training.

Working with the Lawmakers

An act of Congress created the service and other acts of Congress established its parks. Today, every decision, action, and expenditure by the service relies on legislation authorizing it to take action and spend money. So, like other bureaus, the park service must deal regularly with Congress—the government's legislative branch.

Both branches of Congress, the Senate and the House of Representatives, have committees dealing with Interior Department matters. These committees consider bills, or proposed laws, relating to the park service. They ask the Interior Department for its opinion of the bills and may hold hearings on them at which interested people state their views. These might include the interior secretary, the park service director, conservation group representatives, affected property owners, and local government officials. If the committees believe the bills should become laws, they will send the bills to the full Senate and House, perhaps with amendments or changes. For a bill to become law, Congress must pass it and the president must sign it.

Park service officials regularly appear before Congress, which oversees the service's budget and operations.

However, authorizing legislation is only the first step in dealing with Congress. Almost everything—whether repairing a roof or hiring a ranger—requires money. And getting money requires another law, called an Appropriations Act.

Every year the service prepares a budget for running its parks and programs. It submits the budget to another assistant secretary of the interior and to the Office of Management and Budget, which may order the Interior Department and the service to revise the budget to require less money.

Then the park service budget, which is part of the president's budget, goes to Congress, where subcommittees hold hearings about park service and other bureau budget requests. After its hearing, the House subcommittee prepares an appropriations bill for the Interior Department containing its spending recommendations. The House and Senate must pass the bill—perhaps with amendments—and the president must sign it into law before the park service can get its money.

Congress also checks to be sure the park service is obeying the law, managing the parks, and serving the public well. Its General Accounting Office may investigate whether the service is spending its money properly, and committees may make other inquiries. Such investigations may prompt Congress to pass new laws to correct any problems it detects.

Individual senators and representatives often communicate with the park service regarding subjects of interest to their constituents—the people they represent. Citizens write to their senators and representatives to propose new parks, to ask questions about the parks, to see that the parks get enough money, and sometimes to complain about what the service is doing or failing to do. The senators and representatives usually send these letters to the service, requesting information on the questions raised so that they can reply to their constituents. (Of course, many citizens request information and write letters directly to the service.)

Working with the Courts

From time to time the park service must deal with the courts. This usually happens when a person or organization believes the service has acted improperly and sues the bureau.

One recent court case dealt with the rights of people to demonstrate in a national park. A group seeking more government money for homeless people erected tents in Lafayette Park, a landscaped square in Washington, D.C. This action violated service regulations prohibiting camping in any area not designated for camping. When the service tried to remove the demonstrators, they claimed that their action was a form of protest protected by the Constitution and sued the government. The Supreme Court finally ruled that although the demonstration was a proper form of protest, the service was entitled to regulate the time and place of such activity on its parkland.

Working with Other Organizations

The service also interacts with other bureaus in managing its parks and programs. Two of its seacoast parks, Assateague Is-

The Fish and Wildlife Service operates the wildlife refuge within the Assateague Island National Seashore.

land National Seashore in Maryland and Virginia, and Cape Hatteras National Seashore in North Carolina, contain wildlife refuges administered by the U.S. Fish and Wildlife Service. At most of its reservoir recreation areas, the dams forming the lakes are operated by the Bureau of Reclamation, another Interior Department bureau.

Some parks border on national forests, which are managed by the United States Forest Service, a Department of Agriculture bureau. Unlike national parks, national forests are managed primarily for economic purposes, such as tree harvesting, rather than for preservation of their natural features. But both have campgrounds and other recreational facilities for the public. When national parks and national forests are close together, their managers usually cooperate in planning and providing these facilities.

At Lake Mead and other national recreation areas, park management means preserving natural beauty and serenity.

SIX

Managing the Nation's Parks

The park service's primary purpose, of course, is to manage the natural, historical, and recreational parks and resources of the National Park System. In managing the parks, the service follows policies aimed at keeping the natural areas natural, the historical areas authentic, and the recreational areas in tune with the setting and free of the kind of attractions found in amusement parks.

Preserving the Natural Areas

Yosemite National Park offers examples of how the service seeks to run its natural areas. For many years visitors there could see a show known as the firefall. Each evening a park concessioner would build a bonfire on a cliff high above Yosemite Valley, then push its glowing coals over the cliff, creating a spectacular burning "waterfall." The firefall was popular, but artificial, like a fireworks display. Because the park had been established for its nat-

Shuttle buses transport visitors around Yosemite Park.

ural beauty, park leaders decided that this man-made attraction was not needed. In 1969 the service stopped the firefall.

Occasionally, individuals have proposed aerial tramways or cable cars in Yosemite. Visitors would surely enjoy a cable car ride. But this artificial attraction, with its cables and supports, would intrude upon the natural scenery, so the service has always opposed the idea. Unfortunately, however, it has built or allowed concessioners to build too many roads, houses, park buildings, and commercial facilities in Yosemite Valley. Recently, it has begun to remedy this problem, introducing a shuttle bus system to reduce automobile traffic and making plans to remove some of the buildings.

Visitors to the natural parks are eager to see wildlife. In past years, the service sometimes went too far to help them do so. It built pens to enclose animals in some areas, and rangers sometimes fed bears at scheduled times before large audiences. Today the service recognizes that these practices belong in zoos, not in natural parks.

The service once made a practice of shooting wolves, mountain lions, and similar predators who killed elk, deer, and other animals for food. Unfortunately, it eliminated the predators in some parks before it realized that they were necessary to maintain a natural balance. Without them, the number of elk and deer would sometimes grow so large that they would overgraze their natural food supplies and then starve. The service no longer distinguishes between "good" and "bad" native animals, but controversy surrounds some of its current management practices. It

The service tries to remove some exotic animals, including wild burros that destroy the Grand Canyon's native plants.

71

Park employees often allow natural fires to burn.

sometimes tries to control the numbers of some species when overpopulation disturbs the natural balance. It also sometimes tries to eliminate exotic or non-native species when they threaten the survival of native animals and plants. For example, the service has tried to rid the Grand Canyon of wild burros, an exotic species that has seriously damaged the natural vegetation.

Another policy aimed at keeping the parks natural has also been controversial. In the past, the service sought to extinguish all forest fires in the parks—including those caused by lightning. But then scientists realized that fire was part of the natural process by which forests evolve. In fact, the survival of some tree species actually requires periodic fire. So the service now lets most natural fires follow their course, except when they threaten human life or property. Objections to this practice triggered a public education campaign to explain it.

Managing the Historical Areas

The service regards its historical parks as places to preserve and explain the sites and structures associated with important people and events of the past. Few of these places remain exactly as they were—many historic buildings have changed or disappeared, and recent developments have sometimes altered their environments. The service conducts historical research to learn the early condition and appearance of the places and then tries to recapture that appearance by restoring altered features or by reconstructing missing ones. If researchers can't find enough information to restore and reconstruct accurately, these actions are prohibited. This concern for accuracy distinguishes the National Park Service's historical areas from the type of attractions that reflect popular conceptions of history that are not always authentic.

Historical research includes painstaking excavation. Above, workers uncover the remains of an 18th-century tavern.

A good example of how the service develops its historical areas is its work on the site of Benjamin Franklin's house at Independence National Historical Park in Philadelphia. Franklin's house had been demolished long before the service acquired the land on which it had stood. Because Franklin was so important in American history, the service wanted to rebuild his house so visitors could see his surroundings.

Service archaeologists unearthed enough of the house's foundations to determine its exact size, shape, and location. They also found fragments of some building materials and furnishings. Service historians researched Franklin's letters and other records that provided some description of the house. Then service architects skilled in restoring historic buildings examined this evidence and formed conclusions about the house's probable appearance. After all this research and evaluation, the service could have built something resembling Franklin's house. But that wasn't good enough. Even with the information it had, the service could not say exactly what Franklin's house looked like.

Rather than trying to reconstruct the house based on guesswork, the service took a different approach. It marked the foundations of the house and some of its rooms on the ground and erected a steel framework overhead outlining the building's shape. This "ghost reconstruction" gives visitors an impression of the house without filling in all the details, as in an ordinary reconstruction. Historical markers on the ground provide the known facts about the house, and in a modern museum nearby, exhibits and recordings interpret Franklin's life and work.

At other historical parks, the service uses different methods to show visitors how the areas once looked. For example, Fort Frederica National Monument in Georgia was the site of a British settlement established in 1736, but few of its buildings were standing when the park service acquired it. So service archaeologists exposed many of the foundations, and other employees installed exhibit panels with information on the buildings and the

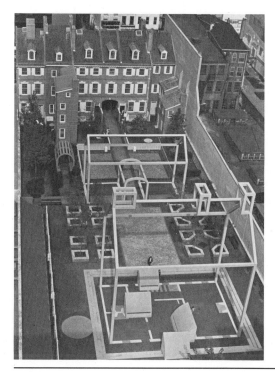

This "ghost reconstruction" of Franklin's home stands in Independence National Historical Park.

settlers who lived there. They also provided further interpretation. Today the visitor center overlooking the site contains a model of the settlement as it appeared in the 1740s. It also presents a film in which costumed actors tell the story of 18th-century life at Fort Frederica.

Another fort preserves and interprets history differently. Fort Sumter National Monument in Charleston Harbor has changed drastically since 1861, when South Carolina troops bombarded it, starting the Civil War. The war destroyed some of the fort, and in the 1890s the army filled half of it with a massive artillery battery to defend against powerful naval guns. When the service acquired the fort, it considered demolishing the battery and restoring the fort to its pre-Civil War condition. But this would have been expensive. Besides, presenting the fort as if nothing had happened would erase testimony of some of its his-

The service opted to illustrate Fort Sumter's history through museum exhibits rather than through a costly reconstruction.

tory. Instead, the service converted the battery's interior into a museum containing exhibits on the fort's history and a model showing its appearance before the 1861 bombardment. Visitors can compare the model with the existing fort to see the changes that occurred over time.

Fort Sumter details how the Civil War began, but Appomattox Court House National Historical Park in Virginia describes how it ended. There General Robert E. Lee surrendered his Confederate army to Lieutenant General Ulysses S. Grant in 1865, bringing the war to a close. The house where the generals met no longer existed when the service began its work there, but unlike the case of Franklin's house, a good record of it was available. This allowed the service to accurately reconstruct the house and refurnish the room in which the surrender occurred. In addition, it reconstructed the village courthouse as a visitor center, where exhibits and slide programs interpret the historical events of Appomattox.

Interpretation is important at most units of the National Park System. It is especially important at historical areas, which do not have the spectacular scenery of the natural areas or the facilities for swimming, boating, and other activities that recreational areas offer. In many cases, viewing structures or settings is not the most effective way to understand and appreciate historical areas. Visitors need to know details about who lived or what happened there, recounted in as interesting a way as possible.

In some places visitors can hear about what happened from people who were there at the time. Visitors touring Franklin D. Roosevelt's home in Hyde Park, New York, can listen to a tape recording made by his widow, Eleanor Roosevelt. In it, she describes the family activities in the house and tells about famous guests who stayed there. At Sagamore Hill National Historic

Visitors to Roosevelt's Hyde Park home can see the desk he used for stamp collecting, and other artifacts from his life.

Old-fashioned, mule-drawn barges carry visitors into the past at the Chesapeake and Ohio Canal Historical Park.

Site, a tape recording by one of Theodore Roosevelt's daughters guides the public through the house.

"Living history" demonstrations are a popular form of interpretation at some parks. Visitors to the Chesapeake and Ohio Canal National Historical Park may ride through a restored canal lock on a mule-drawn barge and hear tales of the old canal from costumed interpreters portraying boat operators. At Golden Spike National Historic Site in Utah, employees reenact the 1869 ceremony marking completion of the first railroad to cross the United States. At several battlefield parks, interpreters in Revolutionary War and Civil War uniforms perform military drills, fire reproductions of authentic weapons, and demonstrate aspects of army camp life.

Developing Recreational Areas

Although some of the recreational parks developed around man-made features such as reservoirs and parkways, the service tries to keep them as natural-looking as possible. It plans development to let visitors take advantage of the natural pleasures provided by the water and the landscape instead of the lures of an amusement or theme park. The seashores and lakeshores attract crowds who want to swim and sunbathe, and they also have hiking trails and other places that provide a sanctuary where visitors can see more birds and wildlife than people.

The service keeps many recreational areas in their natural state so hikers and campers can enjoy unspoiled wilderness.

Planning for Parks

Planning how parks will be preserved, developed, and made available for public enjoyment is an important function that occupies many service employees. It involves research, evaluation of ideas, and advice from the public.

Research comes first. Before the service can decide what to do with a park, it needs to know as much as possible about the park's natural and historic features. It must be sure that it will not build a road or visitor center where it will destroy a wildlife habitat or a buried archaeological site, for example. It must also review any laws pertaining to the park to be sure that its plans will not violate what Congress intended in establishing the park.

After reviewing the laws and identifying the things that will most need to be protected and interpreted, the park planners seek to learn what the public wants. They may hold meetings

Officials hold planning sessions to review proposals for establishing new parks and improving existing areas.

and send out questionnaires so that nearby residents, conservationists, and others with a special interest in the planned park can express their opinions.

From their research and public opinions, the planners may prepare a report with several alternatives for developing the park. For a proposed natural area, they may weigh whether and where to build a campground. For a planned historical area, they may focus on whether certain buildings should be restored or reconstructed. And for a recreational area, they may study various patterns and numbers to determine how many parking places to provide at a beach.

Their report evaluates the advantages and disadvantages of the various alternatives, their effects on the environment, and their costs. The individuals and groups who expressed opinions earlier receive a copy for review and comment. The congressional committees that authorize parks and appropriate their funds may review and comment on the report also. Eventually, the service selects one of the alternatives and seeks money from Congress to carry it out. It may take several years to get the money and put the plan into effect.

The planning process encompasses refurbishing older parks as well as establishing new facilities. As park facilities wear out, as natural and historic features are subjected to new types of threats, and as the amount and kind of park use change, new plans for protecting or preserving older parks are needed. With so many parks in the National Park System, such planning is an ongoing process.

Although the park service's primary duty is to manage the parks, it has a few other functions as well. Most of them involve identifying and preserving other natural places and historic features and helping state and local governments provide recreational opportunities in their areas.

The National Historic Landmarks Program recognizes historic places of national importance outside the National Park Sys-

81

Park planners decide when restoration or construction is needed. Above, workers build a wall at Mammoth Cave.

tem. The National Natural Landmarks Program does the same for natural areas. Some places designated as landmarks later join the system as natural or historical parks.

The national historic landmarks and the historical parks are part of the National Register of Historic Places, another service responsibility. The National Register lists all of the places in America that deserve to be preserved for what they represent or illustrate about America's past. Most of these places are more significant to states and communities than to the nation; an old country schoolhouse, a county courthouse, a local railroad station, and many other things may be listed in the National Register even if they were never connected with famous people or events. A historic preservation officer in each state nominates places to the register, and if they qualify, the service enters them.

The service encourages and helps owners to care for their National Register properties in several ways. For example, it publishes booklets and leaflets that tell how to clean and repair old brick walls, install insulation, and restore damaged or missing building parts. It also helps manage a federal program that gives tax benefits to owners who renovate historic properties instead of tearing them down.

From time to time the service studies the nation's recreational needs and opportunities. In the mid-1980s, it became involved in a study for a special presidential commission that considered how governments, businesses, and other organizations could best serve the public's need for outdoor recreation. In addition, it sends federal money from the Land and Water Conservation Fund to state and local governments to help them buy land and plan and develop recreational facilities. The service can manage only a few of the needed recreational lands and facilities, so it encourages others to share this responsibility for enriching the quality of American life.

The park service maintains the Washington Monument and other national treasures so future generations can enjoy them.

SEVEN

Planning for
the Future

Whren people think of America, they typically imagine its power, wealth, and promises of free- dom and opportunity. But when people think of America, they also think of its diverse landscape—from seashores to mountains to deserts to canyons—and of historical symbols such as the Washington Monument, Independence Hall, Mount Rushmore, and the Statue of Liberty.

Because America's splendid natural and historic features are so vital to its character, they must be preserved for Americans and guests from abroad to visit and appreciate. That is why the government has placed so many of them in the National Park System. That is why Congress created the National Park Service to care for these national treasures and ordered it to present them "in such manner and by such means as will leave them unimpaired for the enjoyment of future generations."

Yellowstone wasn't only America's first national park, it was the *world's* first national park. Since it was set aside in 1872 "for the benefit and enjoyment of the people," many other countries have created national parks of their own. On its 100th anniversary in 1972, Yellowstone hosted a conference of park managers and conservation leaders from around the world. They came to learn how the National Park Service runs America's parks and to share their own park management ideas. Since then, the service has continued to give other nations advice and assistance in preserving and improving their parks.

When Steven Mather and Horace Albright established the service and got it underway, most of the parks were not readily accessible to most Americans. Roads were poor, and only the wealthy could afford cars. Relatively few had the money and leisure time needed to travel to the parks. So Mather and Albright tried to serve more people in order to give them enjoyment and to build support for the parks and the bureau that ran them.

Since then, things have changed. Some say that the nation's parklands are now in danger of being "loved to death." They are accessible to almost everyone, and some famous parks are so popular that overuse threatens their natural and historic features.

Now the service faces the difficult task of minimizing the heavy impact of visitors on these areas. It must limit the number of people venturing into the back country in some parks in order to protect the wilderness and the wilderness experience of those who enter. And in the future it may need to set even further limits on public use. Meanwhile, the service is trying to reduce crowding in popular parks by encouraging people to visit its less known and less crowded areas. Kings Canyon National Park in California, for example, has spectacular scenery rivaling that of Yosemite Valley, with many fewer visitors to create traffic jams and compete for campsites.

The park system probably won't grow much larger: Few qualified areas remain available, and restraints on federal spending may limit park funds. This makes it even more important to spread public use more evenly among the existing parks.

The service encourages people to visit lesser-known parks, such as spectacular Kings Canyon.

The service is still devoted to serving people, as it was under Mather and Albright. But it has learned that its parks can serve only a limited number of people well. William Penn Mott, Jr., who became the bureau's director in 1985, said that when development to accommodate more visitors conflicted with preservation, he would decide in favor of preservation. In the next century, as the population grows, the service will face increasing pressure for such development from all who love the national parklands. To accomplish both development and preservation of the parks, the National Park Service will need the support of those who love them most.

GLOSSARY

Executive branch—The branch of the government that deals with presidential responsibilities.

Exotic species—Animals or plants not native to an area.

Ghost reconstruction—Construction that suggests the appearance of a historical building without completely rebuilding it.

Interpretation—Explanation of items or events occurring in National Park Service areas.

Living history demonstrations—Reenactments of historic events performed by costumed park service employees.

National historical parks—Large areas with sites of historic importance.

National historic sites—Single features of historical significance.

National monuments—Items, either natural or man-made, of national importance.

National parks—Large land areas with spectacular natural features and wilderness.

National preserves—Parklike lands that allow hunting and trapping of animals.

SELECTED REFERENCES

Albright, Horace M., as told to Robert Cahn. *The Birth of the National Park Service: The Founding Years, 1913–33*. Salt Lake City: Howe Brothers, 1985.

Conservation Foundation. *National Parks for a New Generation: Visions, Realities, Prospects*. Washington, D.C.: Conservation Foundation, 1985.

Everhart, William C. *The National Park Service*. Boulder: Westview Press, 1982.

Foresta, Ronald A. *America's National Parks and Their Keepers*. Washington, D.C.: Resources for the Future, 1984.

Garrison, Lemuel A. *The Making of a Ranger: Forty Years with the National Parks*. Salt Lake City: Howe Brothers, 1983.

Mackintosh, Barry. *The National Parks: Shaping the System*. Washington, D.C.: National Park Service, 1985.

National Park Service. *The National Parks: Index 1985*. Washington, D.C.: U.S. Department of the Interior, 1985.

Shankland, Robert. *Steve Mather of the National Parks*. 3rd ed. New York: Alfred A. Knopf, 1970.

Swain, Donald C. *Horace M. Albright and Conservation*. Chicago: University of Chicago Press, 1970.

Wirth, Conrad L. *Parks, Politics, and the People*. Norman, Okla.: University of Oklahoma Press, 1980.

INDEX

national historic landmarks 43,
47, 53, 81
national historic sites 19, 42–43,
47–48
national lakeshores 19, 49
national military parks 19, 36
national monuments 19, 26–29,
36
national natural landmarks 53, 82
national parkways and scenic
trails 19, 44
national preserves 50
national recreation areas 19, 41,
43–44, 49
National Register of Historic
Places 57, 82–83
national rivers 19, 49
national seashores 19, 45
Natural Bridges National
Monument 35
New River Gorge National River
49
Noatak National Preserve 53
North Cascades National Park 49

O
offices, park service 57
O'Neill, Eugene 48
Organic Act 30, 33
organization 55–67
Ozark National Scenic Riverways
49

P
Padre Island 45
Park Restoration and
Improvement Program 53
Pearl Harbor, Hawaii 48
Petrified Forest 27, 28, 31
Philadelphia 19, 43, 74
Pictured Rocks 49

planning 80–87
Poe, Edgar Allen 48
Point Reyes 45

R
Rainbow Bridge 27
Redwood National Park 49
Rio Grande Wild and Scenic River
49
Rockefeller, John D. Jr. 36
Rocky Mountain National Park 25
Roosevelt, Franklin D. 37, 38, 77

S
Sagamore Hill National Historic
Site 43, 77–78
Sandburg, Carl 48
Saugus Iron Works National
Historic Site 48
Sequoia National Park 24, 30
Shenandoah National Park 35, 37,
44
Shiloh National Military Park 38
Sleeping Bear Dunes 49
Springfield Armory National
Historic Site 48
Statue of Liberty 17, 19, 38

T
tourists 22, 24, 46–47, 86–87
Tuskegee Institute National
Historic Site 49

U
Udall, Stewart L. 53
U.S.S. *Arizona* Memorial 48
U.S.S. *Constitution* 48

V
Valley Forge, Pennsylvania 48

Barry Mackintosh currently works as bureau historian for the National Park Service and has held related positions there since 1965. His publications include books about the national parks and Booker T. Washington, as well as articles about George Washington Carver. He holds an M.A. from the University of Maryland.

Arthur M. Schlesinger, jr. served in the White House as special assistant to Presidents Kennedy and Johnson. He is the author of numerous acclaimed works in American history and has twice been awarded the Pulitzer Prize. He taught history at Harvard University for many years and is currently Albert Schweitzer Professor of the Humanities at the City University of New York.